Start an Online Record label

Steps, Insights and Strategies

http://www.musicmarketingrescue.com

Table of Contents

Introduction

I want to thank you and congratulate you for buying this book, *"Start a record label online"*.

This book contains proven steps and strategies on how to start and grow a label online. Your record label is just like any other business venture. Thus, you need to be very careful when starting and running it. This book gives you all the insights on how to start your own record label, sign artists, make your music, market the music and merchandise your label.

Thanks again for downloading this book, I hope you enjoy it!

Chapter 1 Setting up the business

Running an independent record level is fun, but it takes a lot of commitment and investment. Before you leap into the business, make sure you understand what you are getting yourself into. Find out what you need to have in place before you start planning for the first release.

You may want to start a record label for a couple of reasons. First, your may start a record label if you want to release your own music or if you believe in a record and think it's worth releasing. You may also start your own label if other labels have rejected your music and you still believe your product is sellable. Here is what you need to consider when setting up the business.

Home base vs. office rent

The place where you will operate from is very important. Just like any other type of business, your premises should be easily accessible. After hearing your music, fans will come looking for the place where they can get your products. Thus, you need to make the place as accessible as possible. You can either operate from your home or rent an office. Setting up your business at home is beneficial because you do not have to pay for commercial premises. Having a home based business will also allow you to work for long hours. You can grow your home business by making full use of technology to reach customers and generate more profits. However, setting up your business at home may disrupt your family life. Being a music producer, you may need to play loud music which may disturb your kids and your neighbors as well. Also, your customers may not be able to get access to your products if your home is far away from the city. You also need to consider the space needed to set up the business. If you realize your home is not ready for the business, then it is wise to explore other alternatives like office rent. Finding a commercial place to set up your office is a good option if your home cannot accommodate your business. This can also be a great marketing idea especially if the office is set up in a busy commercial area. Renting an office comes at a cost that most start-ups may not afford. Therefore, you need to evaluate your business plan before settling for this option.

Financing

Money, money, money, this is what you need to think about before setting up your business. If you don't have enough to start your business, you need to convince other parties that your label will be a success for them to invest in it. You may ask for financing from your family, friends and business associates. You can also look for money from banks. Most banks will ask for a business plan to find out if your business is viable. Your plan should show the financial estimations and the expected returns from your business. By working out the amount of money you need to cover the business and personal expenses, you can decide on the price of your record. Banks will not loan you money if you have bad credit. You may also find it difficult accessing loans if you don't have assets to attach as collateral. It is possible to start your record label with your savings. It doesn't take much capital investment to start a record label. However,

15

you need more investments to market and promote your first record.

Business form; LLC or DBA

Choosing the right business formation has far-reaching repercussions. The type of regulations encountered, your personal liability and how you pay taxes are dependent on the form of your business. Limited Liability Company (LLC) is one of the most popular business forms. One of the advantages of starting a LLC is the tax flexibility this business presents to owner(s). Members of the LLC determine if they want to be taxed as single members, partners or file their returns as a corporation. In their agreement, members of LLC outline how the LLC will be treated for tax purposes. LLCs also protect their members from liability and present less paperwork to the owners. On the downside, LLCs are usually subject to self-employment taxes. Also, LLCs have limited life. If one member departs, the business ceases to exist unless this was addressed in the operating agreement. You may also consider starting a DBA. DBA (Doing Business As) also known as sole-proprietorship is a form of business where the owner operates a business with a different name. This business is easy to start and maintain. However, the owner is personally liable to the company and its debt. This type of business is only recognized in your city/county and not at state level.

More info and help to decide which structure for your business here (3 steps process): https://www.legalzoom.com/

Sound recording copyright

It's not important to focus on that part yet until you have an official release or licensed a track. Just know that you obtain automatic copyright at the moment you are recording the song (under the 1976 Copyright Act, a work is automatically protected by copyright once it is created). Registering your work will allow you to establish a public record of the copyright claim. Timely registration can also protect you from copyright infringement. To register your sound recording, you need three things; a non-refundable filing fee, a non-refundable deposit and a completed application form. You can register your label manually or online. Online registration is always fast and convenient. This registration is done through electronic Copyright Office (eCO). Online filing fee is lower than manual filing fee. You can also track the processing status after application. The other option for filing for registration of your sound recording is by using paper form SR. These forms can be accessed those forms from Copyright Office website.

You can also use LegalZoom services to protect your works. They will help you fill the application and you'll just have to answer a few question for that (it is a 3 steps process).

Collection

As a label you will need to get a license from the HFA. The Harry Fox Agency is a provider of rights management and collector and distributor of mechanical license fees on behalf of music publishers in the United States. With the proper license, label can sell records with an original song or a cover version. Labels pay a mechanical royalty rate of 9.1 cents per song, per unit (the 'statutory rate').

Create a WordPress website

A website is essential for the success of any business. Your business is like a calling card. It is the place where most people will get the first impression of your business. Designing and then creating a new website for your business can be a daunting task. WordPress is one of the tools you can use to sell your products online. WordPress has plug-ins that allows users to easily build e-commerce sites. You can use this site to create your small business website. You can customize content on this site and assign them your own fields and options. Customers can view your website on mobile devices such as tablets and smart phones. The WordPress themes using responsive design makes it possible for customers to view content on these devices. WordPress based websites can be redesigned to suit users specifications. Users can also add widgets to add functionality.

Find a host

There are many web hosting companies out there. The type of host you choose will determine how successful your business will be. A good host should offer a solid e-commerce tool, a well-designed interface and a reliable site that users can access. You can either go for free or paid web hosts. Free web hosts are great for small businesses that are starting up. However, they lack key tools that may be essential for your business growth. Most of these sites offer limited storage allowance while paid web hosts offer unlimited storage allowance. Free hosts also offer limited support, place ads on your website and may not let you use your own domain name. You can start with free hosts if you don't have enough money for paid web hosting then move to paid hosts later. There are plenty of places to create websites online such as **http://blogger.com** but I would suggest **DreamHost** . It can be a little daunting to put together a website from scratch if you're a beginner to websites, but luckily they have an automatic WordPress installation script (very easy to use). There are many benefits of having your own website, especially if you want to sell your music online without giving 30% to ITunes.

So on Dreamhost you will have to first choose a domain Name, it is free if you choose their hosting service (Unlimited Hosting for $8.95/Mo+ 1 domain name FREE). I will suggest buying it on Dreamhost since it is very easy to manage everything with their Control panel. You can also work with Godaddy or

Bluehost if you want; they all have an automatic script to install WordPress.

Simply register, follow their process with choosing a domain name (Really try to get a .com domain as people are very used to .com, if it not available picks up a .net). As a Label, be careful when come to choose a domain name, simply put **your label's name or your artist name,** don't choose a complicated name. Think to put your name first then a keyword important for your future SEO ranking.

YourArtistName.com or YourNameMusic.com or YourlabelMusic.com

YourLabelCountryMusic.com <<<<<<

Note that if you already have a website for your band, I will advise you to buy a new one if it is not setup like I suggest. It is very important for your SEO. The other website could be used for something else like a blog for example.

22

Ok for now we have a domain name but no host. We need now a place to upload all our files and link it to our domain name. (With DreamHost you will be able to by as many Domain name as you want and you will use the same host: Several Domain and Unlimited Hosting).

When you buy the domain choose their option to host the domain, we will then install WordPress.

2. Install WordPress.

The reason I suggest WordPress is because it is a content management system. It will make your life easier when come to build a sale page or post blog post without dealing with HTML or Flash (you can do many things with WordPress like commerce store, marketing website, single page website....). In DreamHost you go in Goodies and choose WordPress. Then choose

Custom installation. The system will install WordPress for you. Then you will receive an email from dream host in your mailbox with a link to complete the installation. You will have to follow the instructions feature in the email to setup your website. Once your setup is done, go in the Dashboard / Setting and Give a Title for the Website (your website name will be ok), then give a Tagline (Blog of Label Music or My Label Free Music or Jon Doe Music, etc...) and clicks save. Still in Setting, go in the menu Permalinks and select the option Post Name (it is way easier for people to find pages after). You can filter the spams in discussion setting if you want it (if you want to moderate or filter message with links). Stay in Setting menu and go in Writing, in the page you will be able to add ping addresses in a box to allow WordPress to notify Update services websites that you post something on your website (PING). They will give you back a ping for each post you create (backlink)

Here is a list you can copy paste in this box:

http://rpc.pingomatic.com

http://rpc.twingly.com

http://api.feedster.com/ping

http://api.moreover.com/RPC2

http://api.moreover.com/ping

http://www.blogdigger.com/RPC2

http://www.blogshares.com/rpc.php

http://www.blogsnow.com/ping

http://blogsearch.google.com/ping/RPC2

http://www.blogstreet.com/xrbin/xmlrpc.cgi

http://bulkfeeds.net/rpc

http://www.newsisfree.com/xmlrpctest.php

http://ping.blo.gs/

http://ping.feedburner.com

http://ping.syndic8.com/xmlrpc.php

http://ping.weblogalot.com/rpc.php

http://rpc.blogrolling.com/pinger/

http://rpc.technorati.com/rpc/ping

http://rpc.weblogs.com/RPC2

http://www.feedsubmitter.com

http://blo.gs/ping.php

http://www.pingerati.net

http://www.pingmyblog.com

http://geourl.org/ping

http://ipings.com

http://www.weblogalot.com/ping

http://www.feedburner.com/fb/a/pingSubmit?bl
oglink=http%3A%2F%2www.YOURURLHERE.
com/

Finally go to the menu POST and delete the «Hello word» message (you don't want people to see this sample message).

3. Plugins: go in the install plugin page in WordPress and choose add new plugging. On the add plugin page choose 'most popular" and install most of all the plugin.

4. Template

Now it's time to install your template, the more minimal it is, the more it converts. You can use the Bootstrap Theme for example.

A good Landing page has

NO distracting sidebars

NO distracting headers

NO distracting footers

BEAUTIFUL typography

MINIMALISTIC design

I will suggest you to use on of the minimalistic free template of WordPress.

Here is a Page you will create with this theme:

- A landing Page.(offer free MP3)

- A Sale Page (Your album)

- Thank You Page (after buying)

- A Blog Page.(your update)

- Contact page

- Privacy and Policy Page (FREE http://www.generateprivacypolicy.com/)

I would recommend to follow the training "Music Marketing Manifesto". **Music Marketing**

Manifesto teaches an A - Z music marketing strategy from the ground up and is the best product for anyone who wants to lay a proper foundation for their music career. http://www.musicmarketingmanifesto.com

-

Build an auto responder to catch email

New subscribers require special attention. You need to engage them immediately because they are always eager to hear from you. You can build their confidence by building an auto responder for their emails.

When they optin for the free MP3 you collect their email. The autoresponder will send your fan their MP3. Some days after the autoresponder will send an email from you with some update of your band or any stories you want to share. Then after a few emails, the autoresponder will send them an email with a link to your sale page (your album). When they buy they will be direct to your thank you page. If they don't buy you can send an email to a page for a discount price for 2 albums (here you can be creative).

There is auto responder online solution that can help you do this. The software automatically sends an email welcoming the new subscriber to your site. These emails can be personalized to include the name of the subscriber (http://www.aweber.com).

Build a fan base

Your success will depend on how well you can build a wide fan base. Creating good music for your fans is one of the greatest things you can do to win over audience. It is also vital to make your online presence felt. Engage fans through social media sites such as Twitter, Facebook and Myspace. Your website can also help you win over fans. Post everything that you are up to on the website including photos of previous shows, expected release dates for your new music, upcoming shows and links social network platforms.

Chapter 2 Seeking for artists

After establishing your sound recording label, you need to sign artists to your label. Most record labels end up with the wrong artists because they fail to consider important aspects when signing artists. You need to note that your record label is a business venture. Thus, the artists should prove that they will offer good business to you. Do not sign an artist because he/she is your friend. You need to use a checklist when admitting a new artist to your label. This will help you in maintaining standards in your recording label. You and your artist will have a very inconsistent relationship. When things are going as planned, your artists will be very happy with your label. However, when sales go down, the artists will put all the blame on you. As your label grows, you will gain more experience and the standards for admitting artists will also go a notch higher.

Where to look for artists

Before signing an artist, you need to believe that the artist is talented. For example if you want to sign a rapper, you need to make sure that he/she is lyrically talented. Singers should have ability to hit high notes while recording artists should demonstrate ability to perform and attract audience on stage. The talent should stand out. Great talents will always earn you great fortune.

A record label's main function is to sign artists who can make the label profitable. Small labels can attract many artists just like the big labels do. However, great innovation and marketing strategy is needed to sway talent to these small labels. The first place where a record label can find new talent is in the live show events. Upcoming and talented artists normally attend these shows with the aim of impressing record labels to sign them. A record label should send representatives to different live events to look for new talent. Take your time to talk to all artists identified. Some could be signed with other labels while others will hesitate to sign with your label. Give those artists your card and tell them they are welcome to work with you even if it is at a later date. You will also get artists who are ready to sign with you. Talk to them and give them a recording contract if they meet your admission standards.

You can also hunt for talents on Soundcloud.com and Bandcamp.com as they are specialized in indie artists.

Your ability to market your artists will attract more artists to your label. Advertise online, send press releases and do interviews to popularize your label. Set up a website that advertises your artists and develop a sound marketing strategy that works. Stick with the same genre and keep on improving recording contracts for your artists. With time, your label will start attracting high-profile artists. You can use profits from your label to attract more artists. Give high-profile artists better contracts than other labels. This will not only grow your label but will also make it popular in different states.

Preparing contracts

There is no standard recording contract for recording companies. Each recording label has its form of this important document. However, most recording contracts are structured in the same way, look very similar and capture the same concepts. Variations only come in during negotiations with each band or artists. The terms of the contract can vary depending on the expected outcome of the contract. This means that even artists on the same label can have different contracts. You need to contact an attorney when preparing recording contracts for your label. Your attorney will make sure that the contract complies with all the legal requirements. This will protect your company from legal tussles that may damage reputation of your label. Either, the attorney will remove all clauses that artists may use to defraud you or dishonor the contract. These contracts should give you exclusive rights to all the artist's recorded performances during the term of contract. This means that your artists cannot record their music with any other label as long as the contract is in effect.

Some contract here :
http://www.musiccontracts.com/record-label-contracts/

Sign contract online

Signing recording contracts online saves time and resources. The power to have artists sign recording contracts online streamline business operations and makes records easily available. Record labels can use these revolutionary services to sign contracts with their own legally binding signatures. The record label sends out contract documents through email using a third-party online signature service like HelloSign.com . This online service allows each party to track progress of their documents. Signed documents are automatically emailed to each party for record keeping.

39

Chapter 3 Make the Record

Recording Funds

The kind of deal signed between recording label and the artist determines who will pay recording fee. If your label doesn't have enough money to cover recordings, you can negotiate with the artists to cover part of the recording funds. This is common with indie labels that don't have the financial ability to cover all the recording cost. In your agreement, you may include a clause that explains how the recording funds will be recovered. For example, you may agree with the artists that you will withhold the sales until you recoup the money used in recording their work. Other artists will agree to cover all the recording expenses and only sign a contract that allows you to market their work. Either way, it is important to note that you are in business and any deal should yield profits. Thus, before you agree on the mode of payment, make sure that it is friendly to your business. If you are running an electronic label, most of the time artist produce their music in a home studio and don't require funding.

You can also raise money on Pledgemusic.com to fund your project. *Let your fans be part of the production / pre-sale process and it will mean more to them. A Pledge campaign is the best way for your fans to be part of your next release from studio to stage. PledgeMusic's platform allows your fans to share updates from the studio, tour bus, or backstage in real-time, which leads to greater awareness around your next release.*

Outsourcing mastering online

When recording your music, it is important to call in someone who is an expert in a particular field. For example, you need to call in someone who is excellent in playing music instruments to do some parts of the song. You also need to send your work to a mastering genius to master your music. Bringing the expertise of a sound engineer will make sure that your music sounds louder, has the right tonal variation and stereo width. Mastering also helps you to create a record that flows from one track to another. There are several online mastering sites that you can choose from and sometimes as low as $5 on Fiverr. One of the major benefits of mastering your music online is that you can track the progress of your mastering project. Just make sure that the mastering site is up to the task. You may ask for referrals from your friends or other business partners.

CD artwork

Your music needs to be presentable to attract customers. The general appearance of music CDs is one of the things you should pay much attention to. To make this work easier, you can use online sites such as Fiverr or Elance. You can post description of what you want on these sites. You will get hundreds of artworks at a small fee. Try to sort those artworks and select the best for your label.

Photo shooting

A good music video is defined by the kind of photos in it. Your recording label should have good cameras that can capture the events well. You need a team of people as well as the actors/performers who will appear in the video. If you are filming inside, you will need a lighting person. You also need a director to be in charge of the shooting exercise. If your music label cannot afford all the equipment needed, you can consider hiring some or recruiting a team that have their own. Plan your shoot before you start. To plan your shoot, you need to assemble all the equipment needed, draw story board showing each scene, list the performers and the number of shots needed, and brief the camera people the kind of work you want. Take your time before taking the shoot. You can also film the bands and artists when performing live on stage. This is a cheaper option of shooting a video for your music.

You can also seek for a photographer on craigslist in your area. There are plenty of students who will do that for a very affordable price. Simply drop an ad with your expectation and voilà…

Chapter 4 Distribution

Distribution is how music gets into shops. Music distribution companies sign contracts with record labels to distribute their work to stores that have an account with the distributor. The distributor takes part of the income from the sales and then pays the record label the rest. Some distributors sign manufacturing and distribution contracts where the distributor pays recording costs and then keeps all the income from the album sales until all the costs incurred are recovered.

Online Distribution

Record labels can also distribute their products online. Online music distribution is cheaper and efficient because more fans are able to get access to the music. Most online distribution sites allow fans to download and pay for the music at the comfort of their seats. Some of the sites that you can use to distribute your music include; Cdbaby, TuneCore and Bandcamp, Reverbnation, and a new cheap and very straightforward one Distrokid.com (my fav).

TuneCore

TuneCore allows you to distribute your music and keep 100 percent of your sales revenue.

You can make sales without losing your copyrights, recording ownership and merchandising rights. TuneCore registers your compositions globally and allows you to collect royalties earned from the sales. This is an easy to use distribution site that can take your music to popular distribution stores such as Amazon MP3, iTunes, Google Play, Spotify, and more for an annual flat rate. This site feeds you with detailed reports on daily sales. You can collect more royalties whenever your music is streamed, downloaded or publicly performed.

Cdbaby

Cdbaby gets your music to online distribution stores and social media sites where your fans can access it. The site can distribute your music to top download and streaming sites; iTunes, Google Play, Amazon MP3 and Spotify among others. This site also tracks all downloads on YouTube and allows you to collect all the revenue from those downloads. Cdbaby can also distribute your music through your website, Facebook and Twitter. They will help you collect publishing royalties and license your music for film and TV. You can earn more revenue from your work through Cdbaby Pro. This improved site allows you to collect more royalties every time your music is purchased in a foreign country, played on radio or streamed on the internet.

BandCamp

BandCamp provides you a rock solid platform to sell your music and merchandise to your fans. The site brings your music closer to your fans worldwide. BandCamp gives you the flexibility to charge whatever price you want for your music. You can also let fans name the price for your music with the minimum chosen by you. The up to instant stats system reveals where your music is embedded, most popular and least popular tracks and places where your music is being downloaded. BandCamp looks great on mobile devices. This means that your fans can stream and download your music anywhere. You can also use the site to distribute your music through social media platforms such as Twitter and Facebook. To build fan confidence, the site allows you to create a mailing list by collecting email addresses from them.

Distrokid:

Distrokid started at only 19$ a year and you can upload as many albums as you want. They pay you 100% of your royalties and there are no other costs than a 2 pro version. One option which you can have 2 bands name and another one for labels. Their cpanel is very minimal and has only 3 pages (upload, catalog, and bank). It is very easy to upload your tracks to online retailers (ITunes, Beats music, Amazon, Spotify, Google Play, Rdio and Deezer).

Chapter 5 Music Marketing

As a Label, it is very difficult to sale music online, especially on download system retailers like ITunes. You can sell music on your website for a better ROI. The idea is to implement direct marketing and try to find the profile of fans suitable for your music niche (jazz, electro, hardcore vegan, etc...):

Find your niche>Find the profile of people who like this niche> built a funnel> bring them to the funnel > sale downloadable music.

Promoting your music can be a tricky affair when there are so many other record labels producing the same kind of music. You need to be more creative for your music to sell. There are different ways that you may use to market your music. Some of those ways are expensive and most independent labels cannot afford to use them. Before you start marketing your music, you need to identify your audience. Your music may not sell if it lands in the hands of the wrong fans. Look for ways that can help you reach your fans. Here are a few tools you can use to market your business.

Landing Page

When used properly, landing page can prove to be a powerful marketing tool for your music.

A landing page is the first page visitors see when they visit your website. These pages should only be used for short periods and for specific calls-to-action (New Cd, Catch new leads). It is annoying for regular visitors to keep having to click-through to your main site. Your sales page should be brief. Don't clutter it with too many videos or music. Make the purpose for this page clear from the word go. If it is a new music CD or a concert you want to inform your fans about, just highlight it in a few, short sentences. For example, watch our new video, buy our latest album or buy tickets for the upcoming tour.

When it comes to running a successful online business the simple fact is that landing page crucial.

Effective LANDING PAGE has its own science. One trade secret that much marketer use is to create separate landing pages sites that point to their main sales sites.

The information give-away technique is another good one. All you have to do is give away something to your visitors. In exchange for this freebie you ask your visitors give their email addresses (that you catch with an aweber signup form).

This is very important in the sense that this should be the primary objective of your site to collect contact EMAIL. With this, you will now be able to send your marketing message to them again and again at no cost.

Testimonials are also great tool for effective landing page. When you talk about yourself, people tend not to listen or go away. But when people without any vested interest in your success sing your praises, the magic begins.

These testimonials can be founded on your Facebook fan or your twitter feed.

Tell the people in your own personal presentation, the stories behind the band, the people around, and some other interesting stories. Here you can talk about your awards and achievements without sounding like a windbag.

By using compelling descriptions, colorful imagery you can quickly make your copy come alive and increase your convert rate at the same time.

Let's recap, to turn you landing page into an effective pre-sells machine you should:

- Give away something (3 exclusive mp3 for example) in exchange for email

- Include testimonials from fans (3max).

- Use compelling descriptions & colorful imagery.

All in all, these tips are some of the best techniques there are when it comes to learning how to presell effectively and there is no reason it should not work with music too.

Again, I would recommend to follow the training "Music Marketing Manifesto". **Music Marketing Manifesto** teaches an A - Z music marketing strategy from the ground up and is the best product for anyone who wants to lay a proper foundation for their music career. http://www.musicmarketingmanifesto.com

Press release

Press release is a common tool used to bring an artist or record labels free publicity. Press release is basically a simple neat looking sheet that provides news to reporters, news editors and other media personalities. It is a powerful marketing tool because through it you can reach many people. Publications made from the news release are also free. You can use press release to announce the signing of a new artist, release of a music CD or any other news

57

about your record label. You need to be strategic when making your news release. This will help you target the right newspapers, magazines and other publications that deal with music news. You may also target other publications that are popular but do not necessarily deal with music news. For example, if you are planning to give part of your earnings from the sale of your CD to charity, local dailies may publish your press release.

Topspin

Topspin is a direct-to-fan marketing platform that allows record labels to sell albums, films, tickets and merch. This software allows you to manage to your fans by making them active, informed and connected. You can target specific fans by age, loyalty, location and purchase history. There are different ways that you can use to engage your fans. First, you can use this platform to compose HTML emails. You may then send those emails to your target audience with a call to action. The software tracks and analyzes your account all the time. Use those results to plan your next move. This platform also comes with exciting customer support for you and your fans. There are experts who can help you in maximizing your marketing campaigns. Fans also get direct help from the customer support. Topspin helps you to sell digital downloads, sell tickets, send emails and create streaming players for music and video. You can also customize this platform and integrate it with your website, mobile apps or Facebook.

More on Topspin :
http://www.musicmarketingrescue.com/topspin-for-music-marketing/

Twitter

Twitter is another excellent platform to get in touch with your fans. Marketing your music through twitter is quite simple. First, you need to have a twitter account. If you don't have one, you can visit twitter website to create it. After creating your account, you need to follow as many people as possible. Make sure that you follow everyone in the music industry including other labels, musicians, music magazines, and music stores and media houses. Twitter allows its users to communicate their message using 140 characters. You need to make sure that your tweets are relevant to the target audience. Include links to your websites or other places where followers can get your music from. Create your own hashtag and include it in your post. Inform your fans when you have promotions, gigs and other concerts. You can also join trending topics (hashtags) to share your views with other users. You will gain more followers through this. Take time to reply to all questions raised by your followers, publicly and through DMs.

More on twitter :
http://www.musicmarketingrescue.com/music-promotion-and-marketing-with-twitter/

Facebook

Facebook is another social media platform that can prove instrumental in your music marketing campaign. The best way to market your music using Facebook is by creating a fan page. This will allow you to connect with your fans and separate your business from personal life. Use your fan page to give fans basic information about your music, artists, concerts and any other information. Ask your fans for feedback and use the comments to improve your label. Your posts should be well thought of to ensure that they don't hurt or annoy your fans. You can also use Facebook to distribute your music by posting the links to your music and videos. Use Facebook to create events such as concerts and gigs and ask fans to attend. You can also run a promotion through your Facebook fan page.

More on facebook : http://www.musicmarketingrescue.com/music-promotion-with-facebook/

YouTube

Online music marketing can also be done through YouTube. To succeed in this, you need to post compelling videos regularly. Fans will be thrilled to see different videos from your label and will definitely request for more if they are exciting to watch. You also need to optimize your music clip titles and descriptions for easy find-ability. Create custom thumbnails for you music to make it more enticing. You should also customize your YouTube channel to attract more followers. The more followers you have, the more views your video clips will get. Your fans love to hear from you. Therefore, it is important to create time to look at their comments and reply some if not all of them.

More on YouTube :

My free ebook for Youtube Marketing as an artist

http://www.musicmarketingrescue.com/music-rights-on-youtube/

http://www.musicmarketingrescue.com/optimize-youtube-best-ranking/

http://www.musicmarketingrescue.com/popular-youtube-musicians-viral-tubetoolbox/

Blogs review

Most video views happen from blog exposure. You can ask a few bloggers to write a review about your music on their blogs. Ask the blogger to post a link to your music at the end of the review. You can also promote your music by writing a comment at the end of popular blogs and then leaving a link to your music after the comment. People will click on the link and sample your music. Some may even download it or request for copies of your CDs.

Private concerts

Concerts are a great way to market your music and connect with your fans. Use concerts to promote your music as well as your record label. Ask musicians who are signed with your label to perform in private concerts to gain more fans. You should also carry with you music CDs and other merchandise to sell to the fans. You can also give free T-shirts, CDs and other products to a few fans. This will encourage others to buy your music.

Chapter 6 Merchandising

Ravaged by dwindling music sales and music piracy, music labels are now turning to merchandise to make a fortune. T-shirts, staples of CD and stickers have become an important source of income.

Types of merchandise

There are different types of products that your music label can order. Music CDs and shirts are generally the best option for most record labels and music companies. CDs are easy to produce and most fans love to have them in their homes rather than downloading your music. T-shirts have also gained popularity in the music industry. You can produce T-shirts with the name of your music label or photos of artists signed under your label. You can also make customized t-shirts for your fans with the logo of your music label and their names. Most fans will buy your merch to show their love for your label. You can also sell stickers and buttons to your fans. Stickers are easy to produce and cheap for most fans. You can either sell your merchandise online, through a merchandising company or during live tours.

Sell merch online

An online merch sale is one of the most effective ways of selling merchandise. To succeed in this venture, you need to follow a few steps. First, you need to have a good web host, domain name register and shopping cart software. Some hosting services provide everything you need to create an online store. You need to establish an internet merchant account to accept online payments. List all the products you want to sell in your store. Include a brief product description and price that is affordable for yours fans. You also need to add photos of the merchandise in the product description. Sign up for an account with an email account newsletter. This will allow you to send updates to your customers about new products. Encourage your customers to refer others and leave reviews on your website. Establish an account with a shipping website. This will allow you to print mailing labels from your home. Check for new orders every day and respond to customer orders in the shortest time possible. You can also use topspin and companies such as BandCamp, Shopify to market your merch (cds, posters, shirts…). Keep track of your sales and ensure that your customers are always served in the best way.

Sell merch on live touring

Live tours present the best platform to sell your merchandise. You can carry your merchandise with you when meeting your fans. When the artists are performing, you can set a table in one of the corners and display your merchandise there. Hire someone to man the table and help you in selling the merchandise. As your label grows, your merch sales will also grow. It is advisable to hire a merchandising company to take care of your sales. Some merchandising companies can even produce the merchandise for you. You need to make sure that your products are of good quality and affordable to your fans.

Online merchandising and fulfillment companies that are reliable and understand the needs of the musician:

http://www.cafepress.com/ (easy way to create an online store and they handle shipping for you)

http://www.zazzle.com/ (handle shipping for you)

http://www.theconnextion.com/servicesForThe Artists.cfm (CD/DVD/Vinyl manufacturing, online ticket sales, and digital downloads)

https://www.whiplashmerch.com/ musician-focused fulfillment company.

(Interesting article from Ari's Blog on merchandising http://aristake.com/?post=44)

Chapter 7 Create a Star

Talent is not enough to make it in the music business industry. After signing fresh talent, you need to do a lot of work to popularize them. Artists can gain popularity by producing quality music. Fans always rush to music stores to buy good music when they hear it on radio or in streets. They will also fill halls and entertainment parks when that musician is performing live. Therefore, it is important to ensure that you produce quality music to attract more fans and make your artists popular. In order to create a big star, you need to get your buzz up. In this chapter, we shall look at the different types of buzzes you need to make it to the top.

Make the buzz online

Learning how to promote your artists online can lead to the biggest buzz you have ever seen. Internet buzz will make your artists popular in your street, city, State and even in other countries. Get your music online at places such as BandCamp, Soundclick, CD Baby, and YouTube among others (Look at my free ebook for Youtube Marketing as an artist). These sites will help you showcase the talent of your artists to thousands of online users. Online buzz could enable you to sell hundreds or thousands of CDs and other merchandise for your label. A site like Bandcamp allows you to sell your CD online, list your shows and connect with people. You can also use other social networking sites such as Facebook and Twitter to network with people. Networking means connecting with people who can help you in marketing your stars and improving your music label. Follow other music labels on Twitter and always check what they are up to. You can borrow from their strategies or even come up with better ones to counter the competition. Facebook can also prove to be an important networking tool. Create a Facebook Fan page for each of your artists and post their music, upcoming shows and any other news about your music. If the fans like your music, they will definitely like those Fan pages and post their comments. Try to reply on most if not each of the comments. This will build confidence with your fans and make your artists more popular.

Radio buzz

Getting your music heard on radio is one of the hardest things to do for upcoming music labels. You either create quality music that takes the city by storm or know somebody in the radio station to take your music there. Once you get people talking about your music in the streets, then radio stations will have no choice but to play your music. Radio buzz is contagious, once you get airplay in one radio, the message will definitely spread to other radio stations. More people will start calling radio stations and requesting your music. This will make your radio buzz bigger. The bigger the radio buzz, the bigger the star your artists will become. Some record labels pay DJs and other media personalities to have their music played on radio. You can go that route if you have enough money to pay.

Fan club

Building your fan club may take long but once it is built, you can count on those people to get your career going. You can start a music fan club by creating your website and promoting it to the fans. For your club to be successful, you need to determine the focus of the club. The club should be devoted to a particular artist or your music label in general. Research whether or not there is another fan club like yours in your town or city. If there is one, you should work on making your fan club unique and more exciting. Make the fan club for every artist official to attract more fans. Upload photos of the artist, music label and live tours. Link your site to other similar fan clubs to attract more fans from those clubs. You need to ensure that your fan club targets the right audience because this is the only way people will appreciate your artists and make them popular.

Live touring and booking agent

Live tours can present a good opportunity to create a music star. You need to advertise your shows to attract more people. You can do this by placing radio, billboard and online advertisements. If your artist is not popular, you can use another popular artist signed with your label to advertise the show. Make sure that your performances are well planned to accommodate all the artists and to make the crowd excited. You may start the show with one of the popular artists to psyche up the crowd and then chip in one of the upcoming artists. Give those artists enough time to express themselves on stage. If the artist is a good performer, they will end up with many fans. Organize more shows in your state and around the country to introduce your artists and interact with the fans. You need to use a good booking agent for the shows. Most agents act as promoters of the show. After booking the venue, they will make sure that posters and other advertisement items are distributed in the town. This will create a buzz in the city and attract more people to the show.

Conclusion

Thank you again for buying this book!

I hope this book was able to help you to understand the process of starting and growing a record label online.

The next step is to actualize the ideas you got from this book.

Finally, if you enjoyed this book, then I'd like to ask you for a favor, would you be kind enough to leave a review for this book? It'd be greatly appreciated!

Thank you and good luck!

Download my free ebook for Youtube Marketing as an artist.here
http://www.musicmarketingrescue.com

Made in the USA
Middletown, DE
17 July 2019